The Hu
of Poe·

Processing Emotions

6/22/18

To Sally,

It was a great pleasure meeting you. The work you are doing is important and absolutely necessary. It's incredible that we have met! I am hoping that Poetry Speaks for us and Huemen House (My Publishing Company) could partner to create lasting positive impact.

Best,
D.t. Huemen

ISBN 978-1-7320070-1-7
Huemaen House LLC
PO Box 540615
517 East 139th Street
Bronx, NY 10454
www.HuemaenHouse.com

Dedications

This book is dedicated to the youth of Harlem, New York and Fredensborg Project (Candido R. Guadalupe Terrace), St. Croix. This book is equally dedicated to my mother, Joyce Richardson, my father, Trevor Simon, my grandmothers, Lucena Harris and Josephine Simon, and my mentor, R.D Snyden. Additionally, it is dedicated to my cousins, aunts, and uncles. Penultimately, this book is dedicated to the friends I've gained and lost. Finally, this book is dedicated to you, the reader. Thank you all.

Foreword

Dear Reader,

I reckon I should inform you of what Processing Huemæn Emotions entails—to give you the opportunity to back out of this reading experience while you still have the chance.

At its core, Processing Huemæn Emotions is a collection of poetry inspired by my processing both experienced and imagined personal and extrapersonal matters.

This book is comprised of 7 main chapters, spanning the 7 categories of human emotions: Anger, Contempt, Disgust, Fear, Happiness, Sadness, and Surprise. The 8th chapter, Huemæn, is a culminating of those aforementioned emotions.

Thank you for your time. I bid you a long life of good health and great happiness.

Sincerely,

Acknowledgements

This book would not exist in its current form if it were not for the advice of my parents Joyce Richardson and Trevor Simon; the illustration orientation tips of my mentor RD Snyden; the revisionary ideas from my editors Maria Lam and Abigail Capers; and the indulgence from my dear friends. Thank you all.

Content

Chapter 1: Anger

She Drew

She drew a knife on me.
My ex-girl called the police.
They arrived.
Questioned me
and patted me down.
I would have been in the paddy wagon
If my ex didn't yell out.

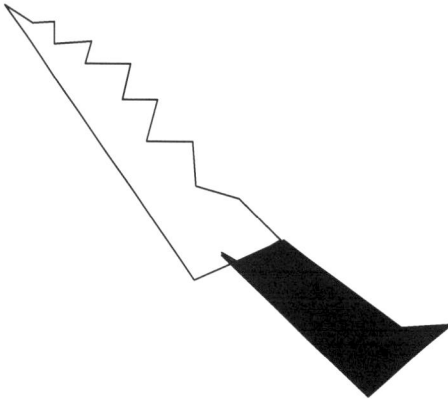

|D.A Huemæn|

<u>Why</u>
Why are we destructive?
Why are we violent?
Why do we lack compassion?
Why don't we stop perpetuating blindness?

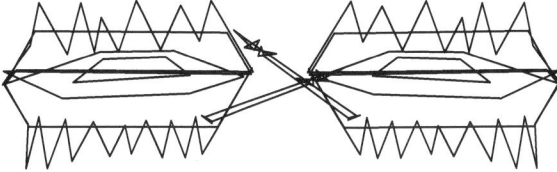

|D.A Huemæn|

<u>She Never</u>
She never came to play.
She came to make a change.
And she will.
Just watch and see.
She'll turn into
The incredible woman
you deprived her of becoming.

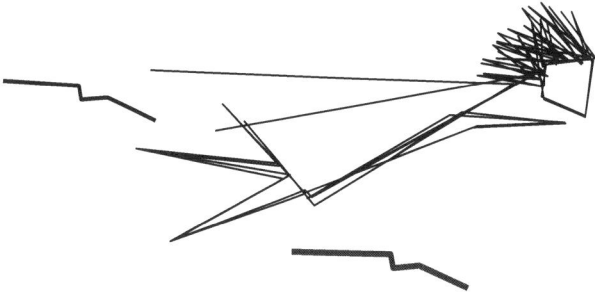

|D.A Huemæn|

<u>In the Hood</u>
In the hood
You were the man if you were the dealer.
These days guys dream to be the fiend.
Fuck clarity. High on anything.
Sip on anything. Dive into anything.
Our time? What time?
We own nothing.

Maybe a few of us do—
Still no dent.
We spend the dollars
Before we earn cents. Nonsense.
We're farmers who eat our hens.
Then sit back content.
Only to think damn,
I should have let those hens lay their eggs.

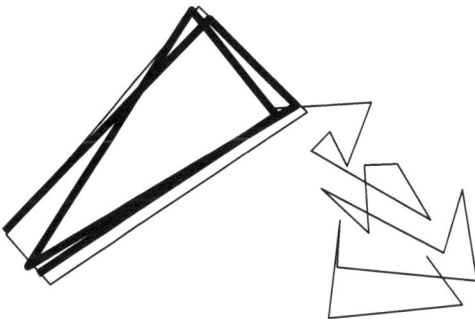

|D.A Huemæn|

<u>Have You Ever Seen?</u>

Have you ever seen a society where
madness is normalized?
In fact you strive and die for it.
It's a society where dreams aren't followed.
Dreams are left to float away like balloons

Then pop and fall in some field
of an obscure commune.

It's a society where citizens strive towards
false successes.
Just to show their faces.
It's a society that striving towards this
"success"
means stick the key in the ignition
of deterioration of mental health.
Starting the engine of a Vicious Virus hybrid.

Vroom vroom
There goes your happiness
from 0-60 in 1.892e+9
Vroom vroom
Let's stay lit down the highway
to nowhere slowly.

Crash if you want to.
The end either way is lonely.
With a special cause of depression.
Hop in this car and drive
Join the millions of citizens
on anti-depressants—
Chasing false successes.

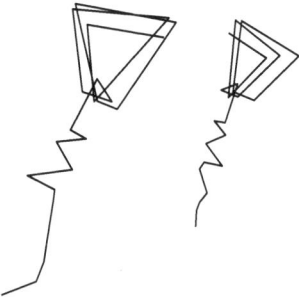

|D.A Huemæn|

Taught Through the Walls
Taught through the walls
Messages of misogyny
Travel through the halls

"Mind your f'in business!"
"I'm the Man! Who are you kidding?"
"Stop fucking bitching. "
"Only your dumb ass would say that."
"Get your fat ass up off your back and do the dishes."
"You're ugly as shit."
"Nasty crackhead ass bitch."
"You're a stupid ass."

"Keep sucking this dick."
"I'll give you something to cry for."
"Lose some weight!"
"Leave me the hell alone psycho."
"Slutty ass piece of shit."

Misogyny kills.

|D.A Huemæn|

Dream Castaway
Her cloudy eyes
showered as we spoke.
The sky closed
as her words flowed.
Absent was truth
through her teeth.
From day one she played
to the sound of her beat.
Daughter of Sega
Dream Castaway
Turned her back
and walked away.

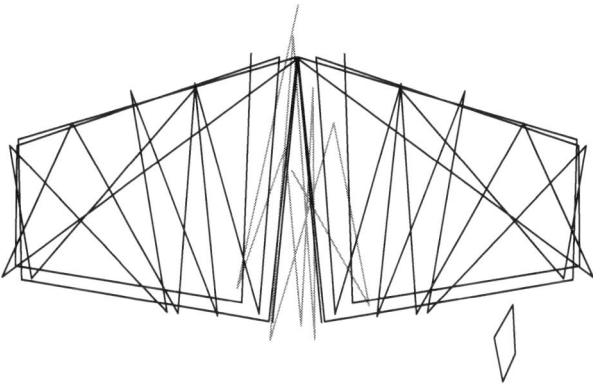

|D.A Huemæn|

A Late Lesson

Everyone tries to tell it.
That's the way of the world.
Her eyes were levees broken
Incapable of emotions.
Ice drum where her heart is.
It's a late lesson
I'm glad I now know it.

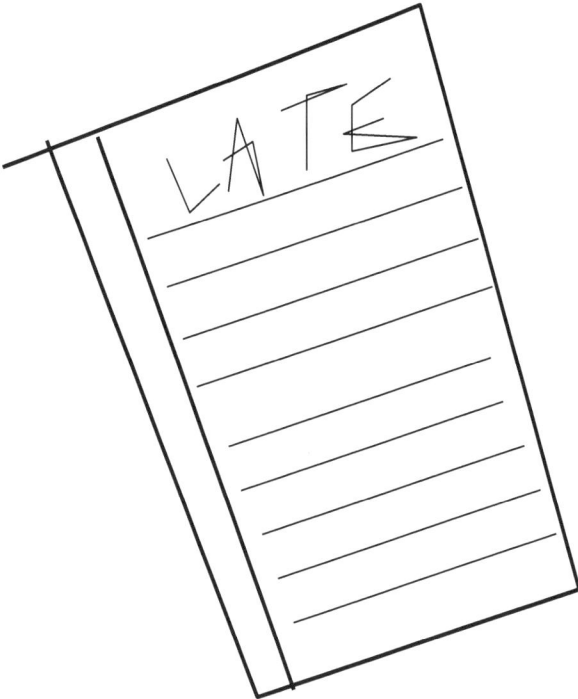

|D.A Huemæn|

March On

March on Sis, march on.
We know life is rough
March on Sis, march on.
We know your husband left you in dust.
March on Sis, march on.
Your son was born premature.
March on Sis, march on.
Your cousin molested you before.
March on Sis, March on.
March as high as you can soar—
And soar as high as you could see.
And seek the strength of your sisters
To survive your past difficulties.
March on Sis, march on.

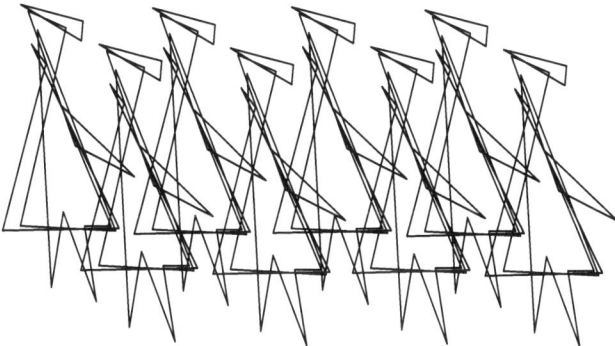

|D.A Huemæn|

I'm Fighting

I'm fighting to the end,
because I'm fighting for my cause.
I'm fighting for the moms.
I'm fighting for their sons.
I'm fighting for the fathers
and daughters living in the slums.
I'm fighting for the day.
I'm sure of tomorrow.
I'm fighting to the end,
because I'm fighting for my cause.

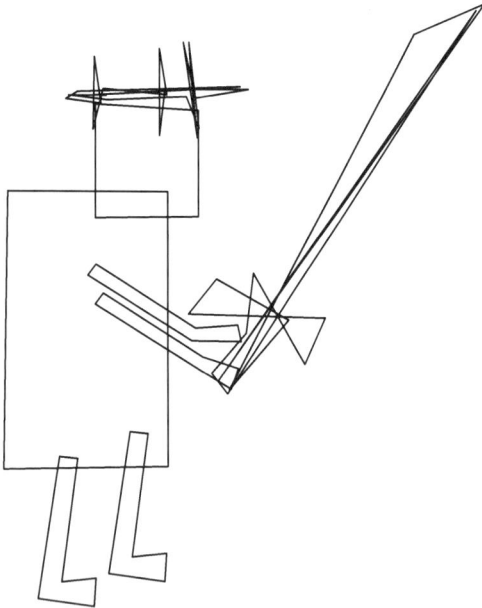

|D.A Huemæn|

<u>Fucked Up Vibe</u>

I woke up with a fucked up vibe.
Yesterday was yesterday.
Still, this morning I am a choleric child.
Today's battle has just begun.
Today's battle hasn't been won.

Thursday's song hasn't been sung.
This fucker just coughed on me.
Okay, strike one.

Shit wait.
Okay.
I'll change my vibe
I can't let the bad vibes
Take over my only mind.
If I do
It's only a matter of time
that I'll be bald and miserable like you.

|D.A Huemæn|

Pigeon Hole

Are they still killing us?
I can't tell.
My head has been in this pigeon hole
Sucking on chicken breast.

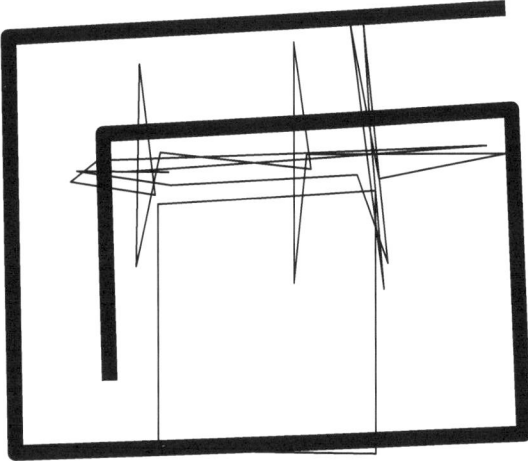

|D.A Huemæn|

<u>I Hurt</u>
I hurt my heart with you once.
Twisting it till it was black and blue.
I doubt that'll happen again.
Hurting my heart fiending for ~~love~~ you.

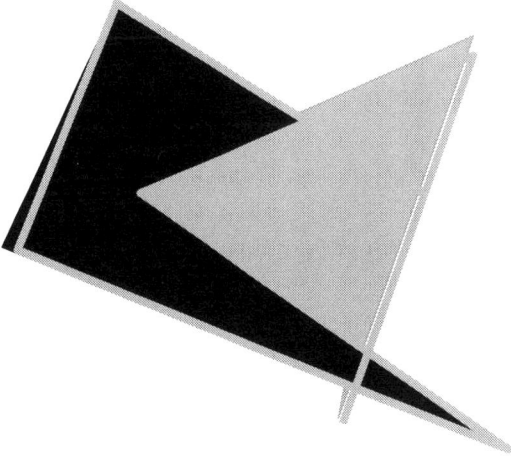

|D.A Huemæn|

The Authorities

The Authoritative Bunch in Blue
crunch numbers
caging us—me and you.
The inhumane non-human bunch
try to snuff us out with
a stroke of a pen
or a slam of a gavel.
We are not caged animals
but great thinkers.
Not cashable checks
but great tinkers.
We are magical people with dark skin
Not caged animals
~~But~~ huemæn.

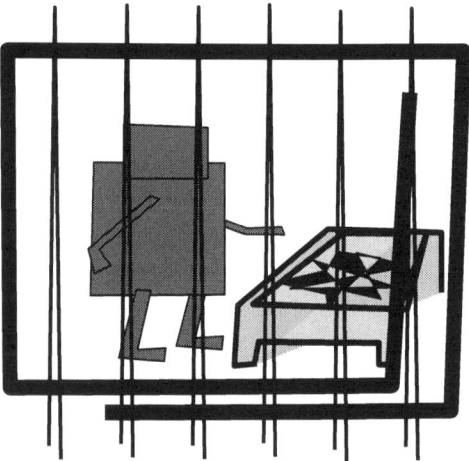

|D.A Huemæn|

Chapter 2: Contempt

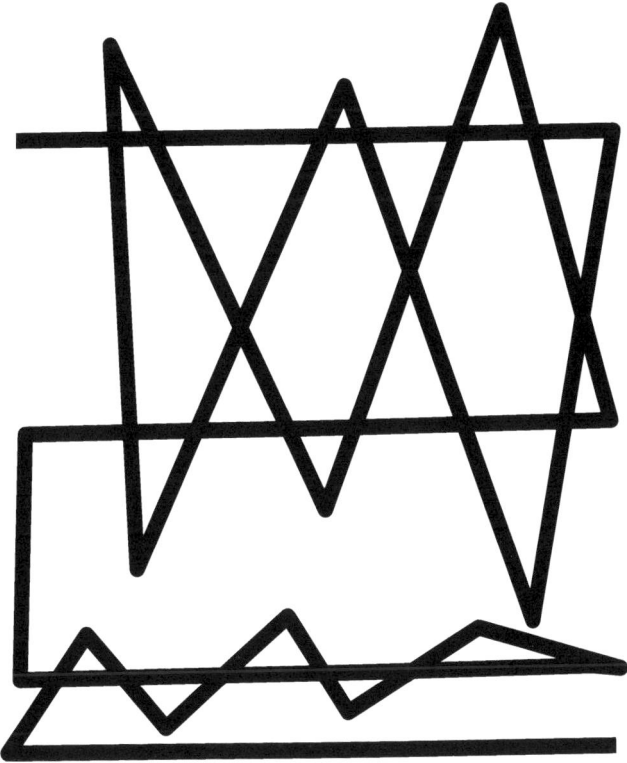

It Doesn't Matter
It doesn't matter anymore.
Leading you is leading me to misery.
Your negativity is poisoning my positive energy.
You can't see it because you're too busy
Looking at yourself in every reflection you see.

I'll tell you
You're beautiful
But you don't believe me.
Maybe if you heal.
And I heal.
Perhaps we can be.

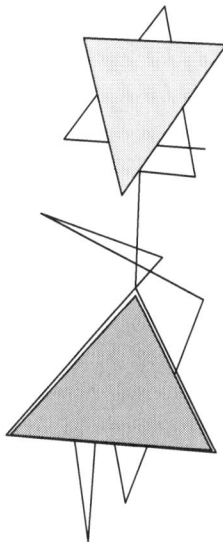

|D.A Huemæn|

Take One
Take One
Take Two
Take Three
Take Four
~~How long can I deny~~
How many times
Will I screw up
The love
That's knocking
At my door.

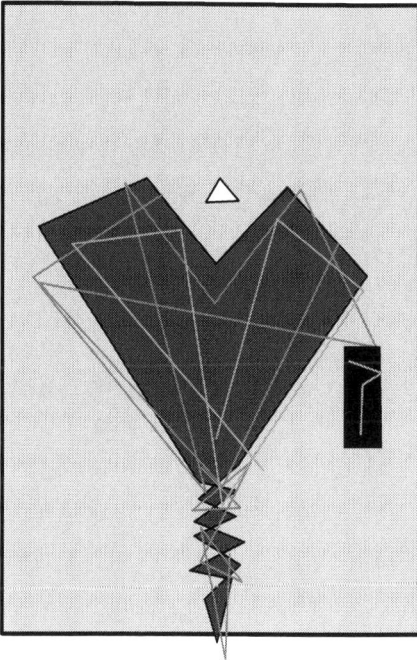

|D.A Huemæn|

Argue

Always we'd argue.
We've both had our hearts filled.
We'd cry and yell.
And yell and cry.
But there's no use in crying
Over spilled milk outside.

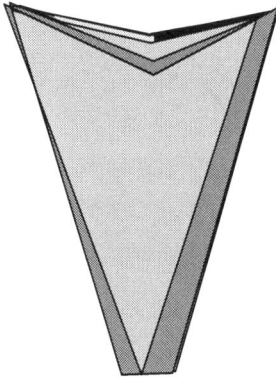

|D.A Huemæn|

Last Night

Last night you hurt me for the last time.
Today I chose to call you Bye.

|D.A Huemæn|

<u>Never Bite</u>
"Never bite the hand that feeds you."
That's what my mom said
when I was 3 years old.
I still remember those words
as though they were a day old
I've chewed carefully
ever since.
These children don't care who's fingers they've bitten.

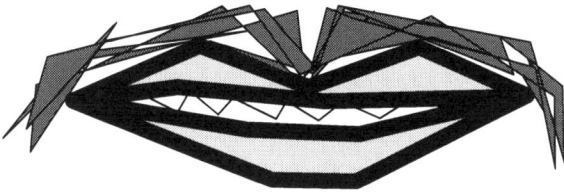

|D.A Huemæn|

Relevant Irrelevance

Don't tell me about anything unimportant.
Don't tell me about basketball, baseball, football, or
soccer.
Don't tell me about boxing.
Don't tell me about love and hip hop.
Don't tell me about the Oscar, Grammys, or the VMAs.
Don't tell me about any of these things.

As long as granny sends you to school
to bring better days.
Don't tell me about Kanye, Kim, or Kimye.
Don't tell me about Big Sean, or Ariana Grande.
Don't tell me about Beyoncé and Jay.
Don't tell me about Stephen Curry.

Don't tell me about his daughter
nor anything as adorable.
Don't tell me about White Iverson.
As long as our black I's versus us.
Don't tell me about lil Wayne,
Young Tunechi, or Weezy.

Even if I'm wheezing to death
Don't tell me about Drake and Future.
Don't ask me about the Illuminati
As long as you're here to illuminate your life.

Don't tell me about sneakers.
Don't tell me about clothes.
Don't tell me about pussy, or boobs.
Don't tell me about milfs, midgets, or hoes.
Don't tell me about anything your dick goes into.

Don't tell me about trends, friends, gems
Jen, Lent, fasting, a dollar, or a cent,
Nikes, Jordans, LeBrons, Kobes,

Wiz Khalifa, Reefa, Keisha,
Christmas, Christian Louboutin
or Christopher Columbus
Neither your mister, nor your misses.
I don't care if you miss her or him.
Ski trips, summer vacations
and spring break are all great
Nonetheless, don't tell me
about any Relevant Irrelevance.

|D.A Huemæn|

<u>What Nigga?!</u>
"What Nigga?!"
That's what my student said
when I approached to help him.

"What Nigga?!"
"Loosen up."
That shit left me triggered.
 I felt like he had just noosed me up.

|D.A Huemæn|

Mr. Simon

"Mr. Simon is a Bitch"

That's what a student wrote on a desk.

That shit didn't hurt though.

That shit didn't even itch.

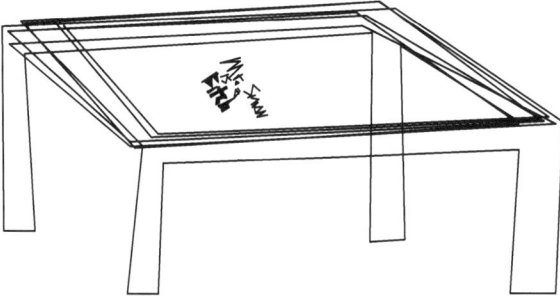

|D.A Huemæn|

<u>Is Ignorance Really Bliss?</u>
Is ignorance really bliss?
Bliss is absolute happiness.

Ignorance is oblivion,
torpidity, and lethargy—
a state of emptiness—almost.

Does blissfulness really come
from emptiness?

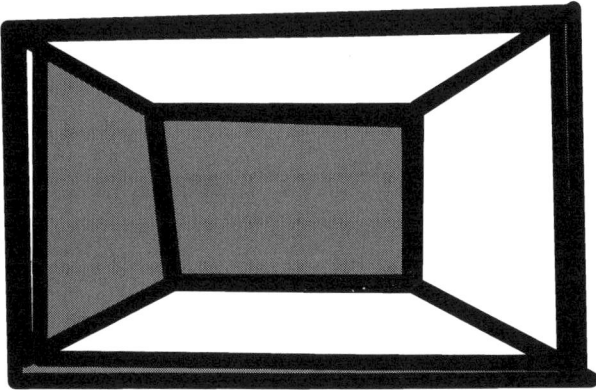

|D.A Huemæn|

<u>Who Comes Back?</u>
Who comes back
only to act like they've never made it out?
Who acts
like they didn't go
to the other side
and saw that the grass wasn't only green
but it is real?

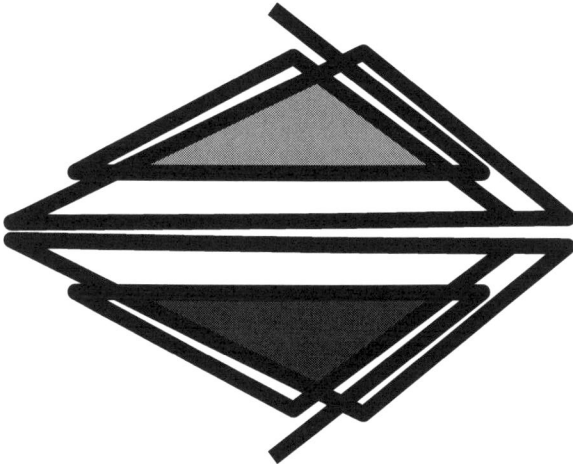

|D.A Huemæn|

<u>You're Bad</u>
You're bad.
Too bad
You lost.
Too bad
Our paths crossed
Never merged.

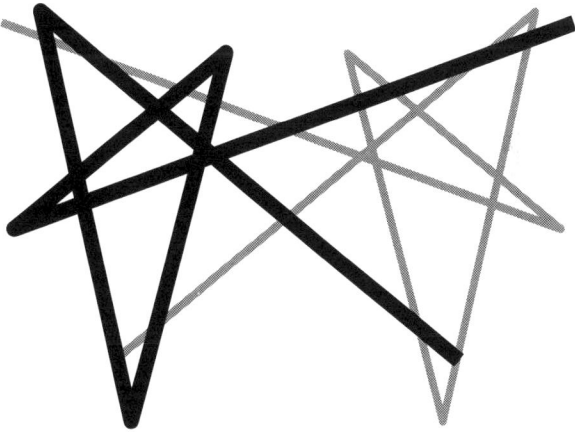

|D.A Huemæn|

I Would've
I would've wifed her.
She ain't care I liked her then.
Now, she's struggling.

And she wants me to lay the pipe in..
Crying all the time.
I put my windshield wipers on
Full motion
deflecting all water off.

I would've wifed her.
She ain't care I liked her then.
Before the 1 nighters turned 2 then 4
Then 8 to 10

I would've wifed her.
She ain't care I liked her then.

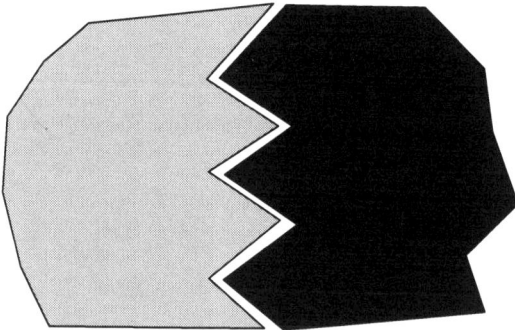

|D.A Huemæn|

<u>Nowhere to Live</u>
Nowhere to Live
Beside our cardboard boxes
And our foldable church chairs
Our baby lotion
Gloves and jackets,
we wear all year—every year
There is nowhere for us to live.

They've taken our homes
Our apartments
Our stores
And told us to go South.
But Harlem is all we know
It's the place of our birth and growth
our memories and our hope.

|D.A Huemæn|

You're Tired

You're tired of me
and I couldn't be happier.
You're tired of me and you seem to enjoy it.
Your introversion is pronounced
best when I'm in the room.
Your sneakiness is obvious.
You're tired of me and I know it.
So let me go
I'm tired of you too.

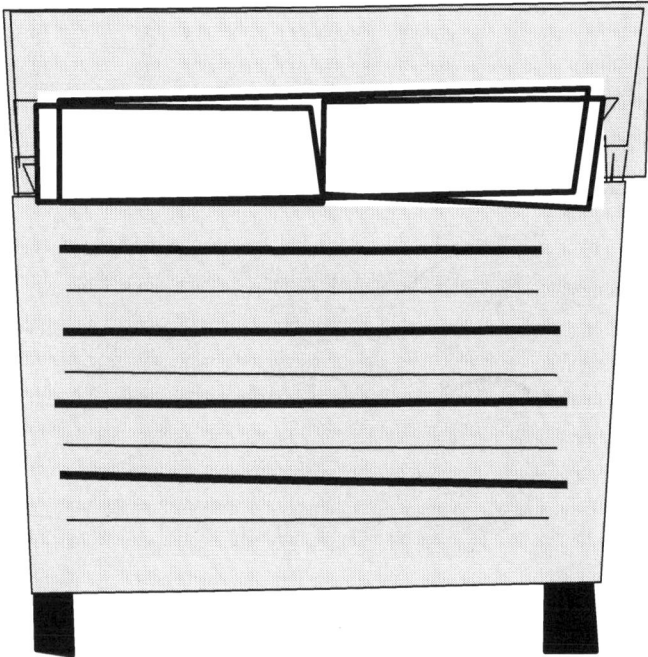

|D.A Huemæn|

<u>Call Me Ugly</u>
Call me ugly
Kid, I don't mind.
Your lunch break was yours
Now that time is mine.
Detention everyday
Until you learn.
Respect isn't given
It must be earned.

|D.A Huemæn|

Opportunity

I had the opportunity
to smash some bad beauties
I didn't fuck.
Now if they throwing
that ass at me it.
I'm still not busting
those nuts.

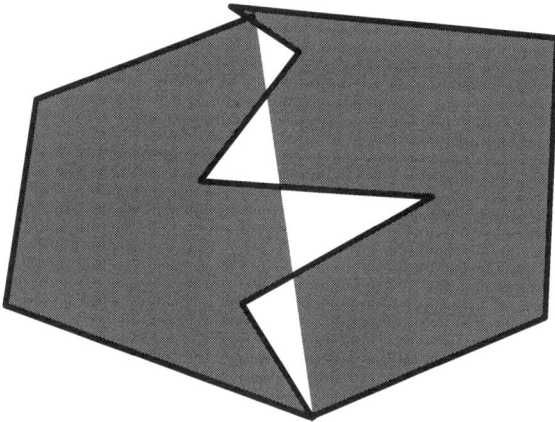

|D.A Huemæn|

Big Ass L

She left me and chained herself to a big ass L.

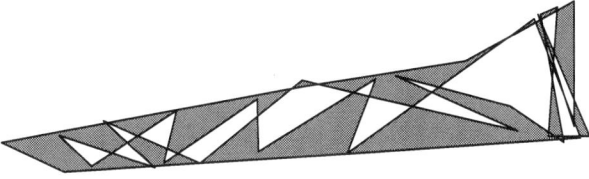

|D.A Huemæn|

<u>Curve Me</u>
If I were you.
I'd curve me too.

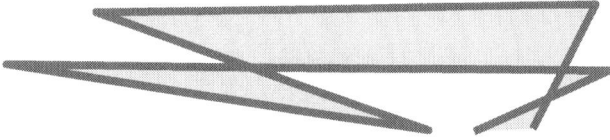

|D.A Huemæn|

Wants

We think we know what we want.
Then we get it.
Then we don't want that shit.

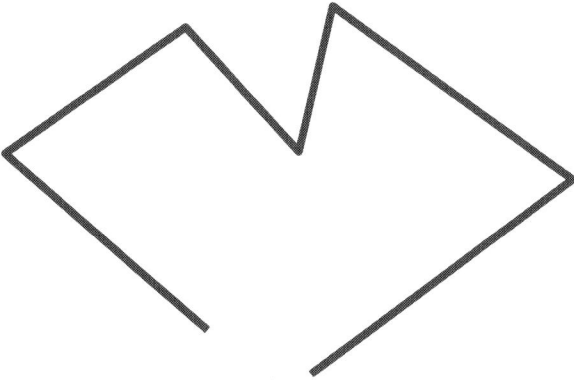

|D.A Huemæn|

Detached

Perhaps I'm way too detached.
I've been alone so long.
I don't get along with anyone else.

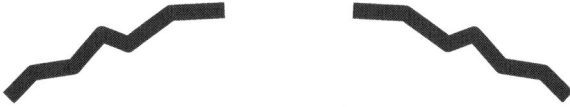

|D.A Huemæn|

Chapter 3: Disgust

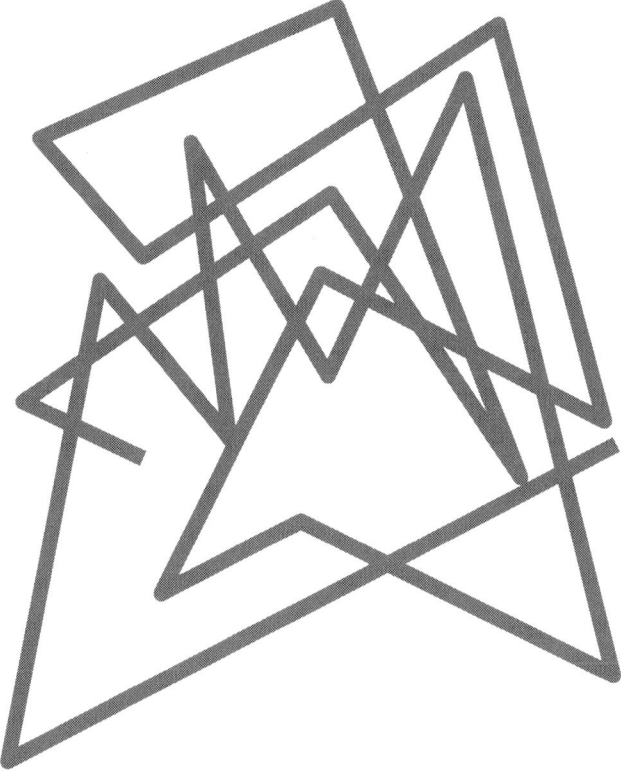

Peaches & Roses

Everything isn't peaches and roses.
In fact most things aren't.
Like the words produced and spewed from
the minds of non-truthers
Bottled lies are sold as truth
Would have you believing
The sky was red
And your head was your ass.
For good reason.
You were born wise
And programmed to be stupid
Everything isn't peaches & roses.
Please know this.

|D.A Huemæn|

Agnostic
Agnostic I Guess.
I am not Jewish.
I am not Christian.
~~I am not Buddhist~~
~~I am not Hindu~~
I am not Muslim.
But if I were
I'd be the door man
Or the floor or chore man.
Religion is a whore man.
Damn thing fucks everything.

Peace,
What does that look like
In a world plagued with divisions
Reinforced through religious fanaticism?
I am not Jewish.
I am not Christian.
I am not Muslim.
Most the world's wars have been
Fought between Abraham's children.

|D.A Huemæn|

Young Man
Young man listen.
You're like 14
Perfect age to be king.
But the songs you sing
The things you do.
Condition you
to be in a cage.
Condition you
to be brain dead.
Dead even!

Yea.
Condition you to be headless
Head severed
Severely chopped off
Gently cut
Modestly sliced
Diced and diced
Your senses melt away like ice
Young man listen
You're my brethren
Your children
Will look like my children.
Young man listen.

|D.A Huemæn|

Now and Forever

Why must we fight Now and Forever?
It is unfair.
We're square up in front of Now—
A Blue Beat Threat.
And like a cloud hovering over our heads
there is Forever—
An unknown.
Now, (it seems) wants to get rid of us forever.
But, like the sun,
We shine through the gloomy clouds
Daring to be seen.
Pushing against artificial weather.
Wherever. Whenever.

|D.A Huemæn|

99 Problems

An 8th grader told me to suck his dick.

Now that's vile.

If I were in 8th grade I would've punched him in his mouth.

My ex told me I ain't shit.

Now that's wild.

Cause when she was with me

She wore me like I was in style.

Now, I can't have these bad vibes slow me down.

In real life I got 99 problems

And not one of them can ever make me frown.

Today I shipped some motion sensor lights to my mom.

(Hurricane Maria has the whole island turned off.)

Then I sent some can goods to my aunt.

(She always worrying but if I'm alive she will never starve.)

After that I put some money on my cousin's account.
Oinks got him in their pen. He'll be out in 5 months.
Tomorrow I may give my grandmother a back massage.
She's been having pain since 16 when she fell off that horse.

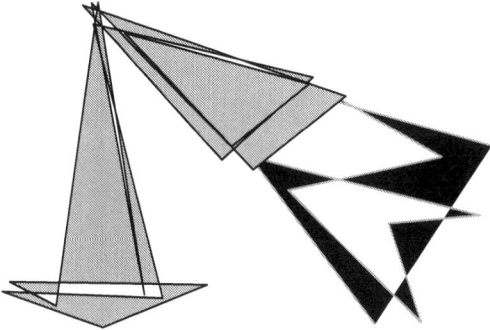

|D.A Huemæn|

Please Enslave Me

Could you please enslave me?
I am always on 125th street
And Lexington,
Selling Crack to a kid my complexion.
He's not the user
He buys it for his mom
and his step dad.
He's fifteen so his favorites are purple and sour
He tells me when he hits it
It takes him high
in the sky like an eagle.
He's my friend.
He keeps the green in my pocket.
Plus his parents are strung.
Every week I put new kicks in my closet.
What's life if you can't get fly?
What's life if I can't kill guys who look just like me?
What's life if I don't ask to be enslaved?

|D.A Huemæn|

Brother

Brother oh brother
You took the life of a son of your mother.
Now she cries.
Through the days and the nights she cries.
With her faith she fights but still cries.
Brother Oh Brother
Why the hate?
Why did you kill the son of your mother?

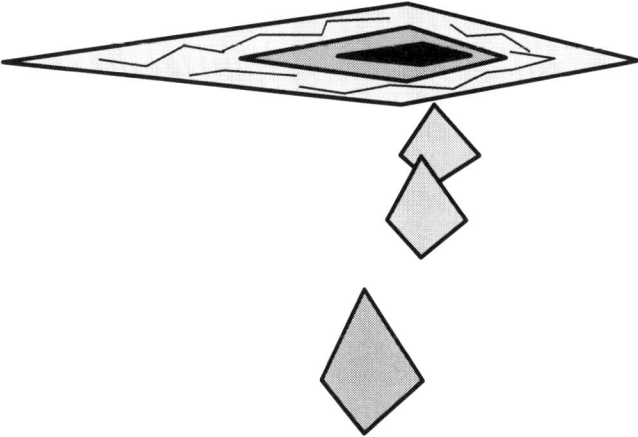

|D.A Huemæn|

The Successful Fail

Those who fail
and blame life for handing them "bad luck cards" by the pail
are like butterflies who land on rocks
then blame the wind for blowing it across fields filled with bright pink pentas
into the mouths of foxes.

To them it stinks.
"I have rotten luck" they exclaim.
Without ever once thinking, it was they who missed their crowning as queens and kings.
These types of people are banshees who predict all the worst things.
And in a twirl of irony they are successful as they fail.

|D.A Huemæn|

<u>Defend</u>
To the person I did not defend.
Please do accept my apology
for being unforthcoming in your defense.

The sexual harassment you faced today
can never be justified.
No justification of any one on earth
or the wisest in heaven will suffice.
You asked for help
but instead you got a hand on your waist
and pelvic thrusts to your ass
Twice.

Such an ass that guy.
Such an ass am I.

I thought he was your husband
how freely he touched you.
Then I noticed your discomfort
and knew immediately it wasn't true.
I apologize for not defending you.
No being should ever be violated.

|D.A Huemæn|

<u>Who Are They?</u>
Who are they?
What are they here for?
And why do they have to stay?

They've come to help us
Many molest us
Who are they

Who are they?
How could they do this?
Our bodies are not theirs.

Who are they?
Why do they hate us?
We are human too.

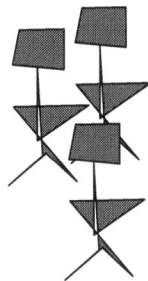

|D.A Huemæn|

Live Here

Why Do You Live Here?
You live here because you can.
I live here because I can live nowhere else.

|D.A Huemæn|

Green Scheme

I hope everything is legitimate.
I hope everything is real.
I hope you make your money.
I hope it truly is green.
I hope everything is legitimate.
I hope there is no scheme.
I hope you make your money.
I hope it truly is green.

|D.A Huemæn|

In My Hood

In my hood there's a lot going on.
Slap boxing matches
Organs being trafficked
Sexes being played with
Men emasculated

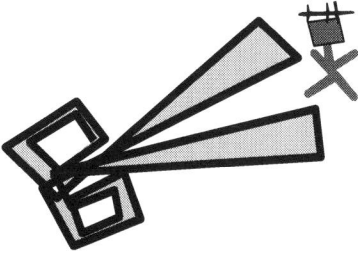

Music blaring
Bitch ass ops staring
5 year old swearing
at 55 year olds
15 year olds playing hard like they're O.Gs
Self-important graduates
Humble bragging activists

Activated cups of disillusioned rappers
Fake ass trappers
Military bastards
Porn magazines
next to my children's Snapple
Guns Kush and Backwoods
Coke cane and acid

Rastas Muslims and Catholics
Poppa's Bentley
Sons with no bus passes

In my hood there's a lot going on.
There's a lot of fakeness
1800.91.Fraud
100% fake
Like the Gucci Louis whatever
we rocking these days.
Valuing dumb shit
Then we act like we made.
We worship our selves
Then act like we saved.
In my hood there's a lot going on.
I'm just try to make it better
Someway somehow.

|D.A Huemæn|

<u>Famous</u>
A famous friend of mine
Tried to bribe me with our friendship.
I laughed and said famo the ship's been sinking.

|D.A Huemæn|

Turn Villain

Take her out to dinners.
Play with her 3 children.
She wants me as her man
Now that her dream guy turned villain.
I say no.
I'm Villain.

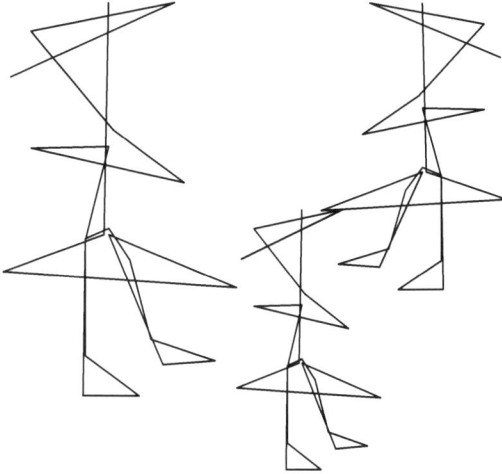

|D.A Huemæn|

Ridiculed
You ridicule me for being for you.
Now you want me and can't get close.

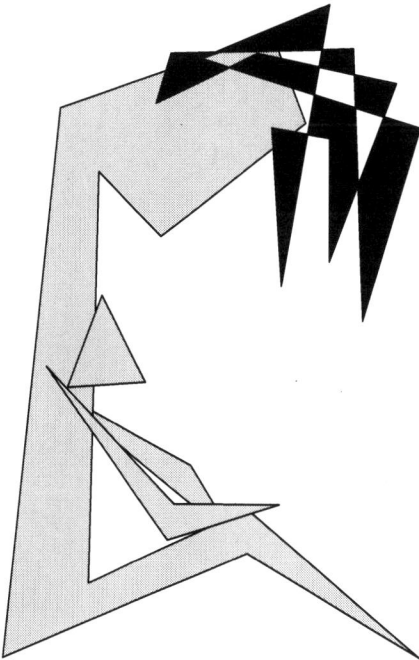

|D.A Huemæn|

<u>Say to You</u>
I don't know what to say to you.
I thought of you so much
The sight of you
 makes me uncomfortable.

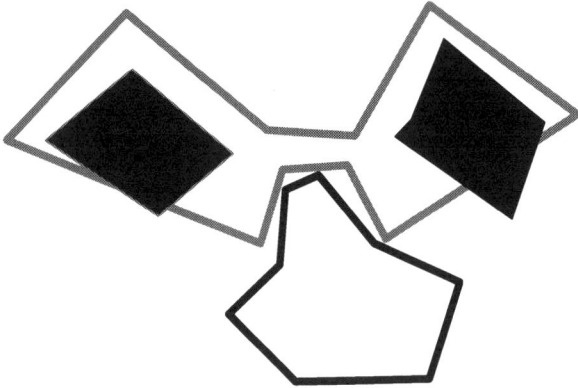

|D.A Huemæn|

<u>Whipped</u>
I hit it and got whipped.
You hit me with
You don't do relationships.
Now I'm up a little
You want that shit.

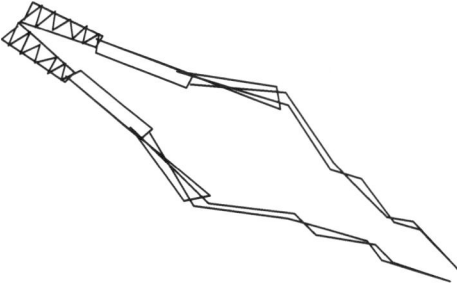

|D.A Huemæn|

Pushed You

I pushed you down to lift me off.
It was as simple as a nut.

|D.A Huemæn|

<u>Greed</u>
Is always wanting a woman and a half.
So much so
We'd trade to get the half
With the woman that we have.

|D.A Huemæn|

Lame Shit

I've judge people for the lamest shit.
That shit dangerous.

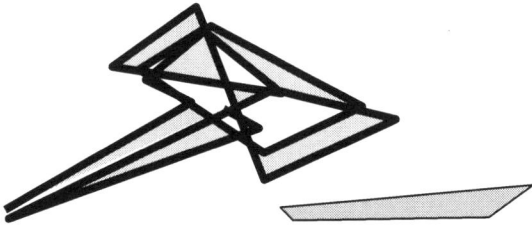

|D.A Huemæn|

Hungry & Humble

Hear the monster grumble
Tummy tucked in
Without surgery
Both are sins honestly.

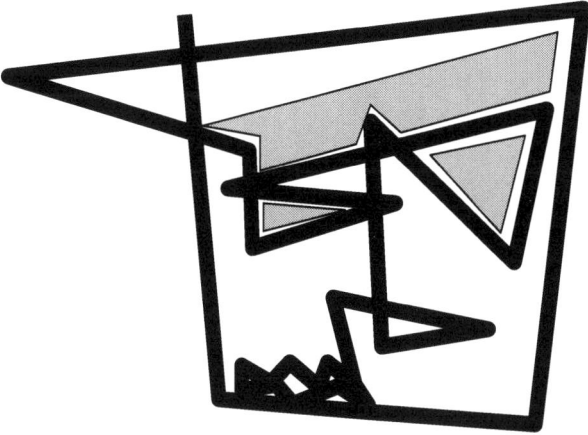

|D.A Huemæn|

Chapter 4: Fear

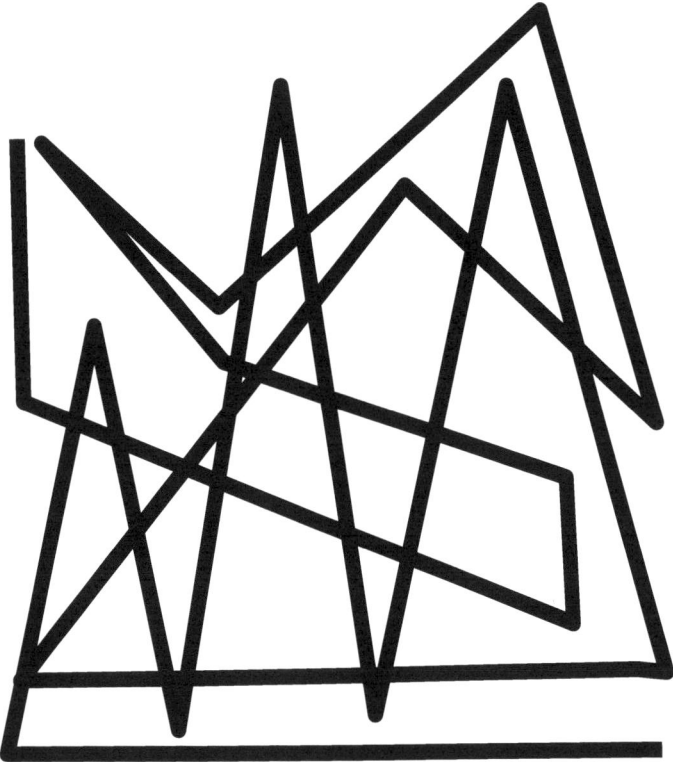

My Mind Wanders

My mind wanders
Sometimes.
My thoughts drift away
Floating infinitely through space
Never colliding with anything
Just shapeshifting
making its way through
dark places.

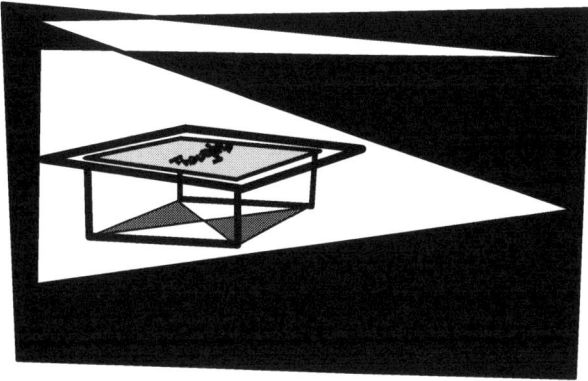

|D.A Huemæn|

I Never Sleep
I never sleep.
I wish I could.
I close my eyes
And count to five
Yet, wide awake am I.
I never sleep.
That's no surprise.
Maybe I'll sleep
When I close my eyes of life.

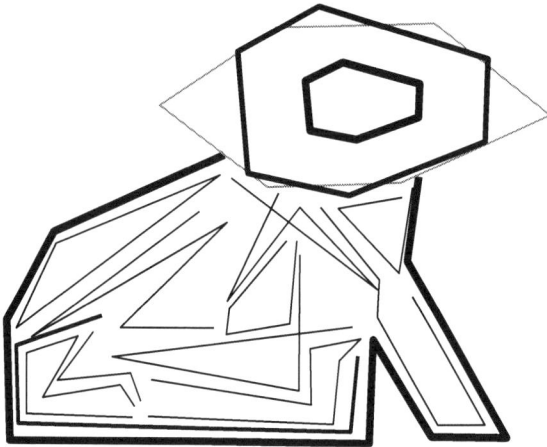

|D.A Huemæn|

Still Life
Crracc
Póp Póp Póp
Shoot shoot shoot
Oh shoot they're shooting!
Am I shot?!
Call the police please.
Call 911
Nigga for what?
Nigga! Them the cops!

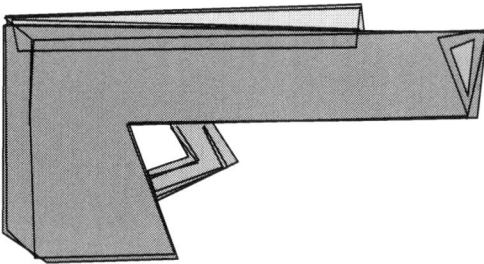

The operator been knew
What the hell was up
Before the shots rang out.
Black man put down
Like a sick hound.
Black gun gold badge
Those the devil's tools.
The whole police force
is who the devil screws.
Latest incident

But the shits not news.
This shit ain't new
Same shit.

No toilet.
Like days when we shat in holes
This is great great great
Great great great
Grand daddy old.
6 generations of grand daddies long gone.
They been got killed.
They not dead.
They life not still.
Their souls too real.
Their bodies were stole.
But their souls?
Those blood thirsty
No heart barbarians
Could not steal.
Still Life
Crracc
Póp Póp Póp
Shoot shoot shoot
Oh shoot they're shooting
Am I shot?!

|D.A Huemæn|

Fireworks with No Color

Firework with no colors
Fireworks at three in the morning
No color
Just noise at three in the morning
Metal hitting the pavement
Is a bad sign of shell casings.
Fireworks with no colors
A troublesome combination

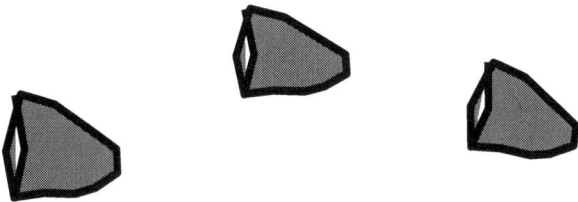

|D.A Huemæn|

When Those Guys Speak

Tears when those guys speak.
It seems as though
they have no appreciation for life.
It seems as though
they believe life is guaranteed.
As if...
As if life lasts forever
As if...
As if they would
definitely be able to shimmy
Themselves out of
the grime of these gritty streets.
Tears when those guys speak.

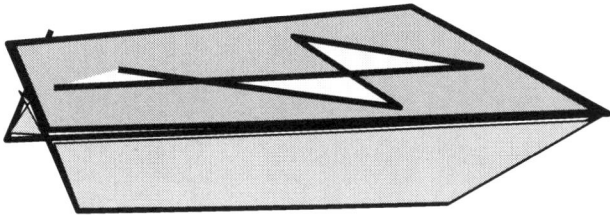

|D.A Huemæn|

Burning the Rubble

The arsonist said what the heck
Just burn the rubble.
Those people are useless anyway.
So burn the rubble.
Burn them until the redness touches the heavens.
Burn them down!
Burn them now!
Burn the rubble.
Until those starving people are scared
to have their bellies grumble.
Burn the rubble
It has become nothing but trouble.

|D.A Huemæn|

From this Place Called Harlem

From this place called Harlem
Where the birds don't sing.
Where the youth are abused
And some kids catch strays.
It's no wonderland,
No wonder officers get raises
And lawyers live well
Since there's always new cases.
Same old charges but different faces.
Old ass apartments,
In the sketchiest places
Our kids are pacing on the block.
They're brain dead.
Red eyes—Satan's
It's no secret they treat the street life sacred.
Simply trying to survive this matrix.

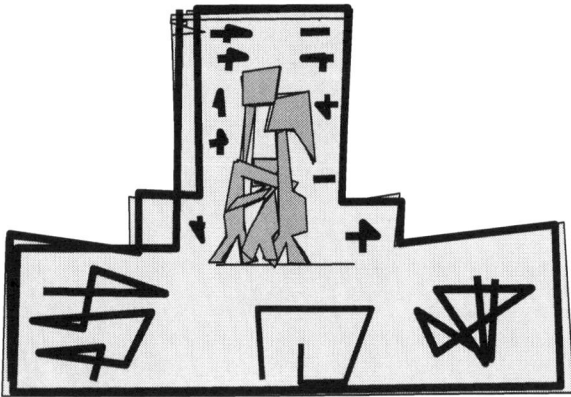

|D.A Huemæn|

Color

The color of our skin
makes us so prone to injustice.
Stop and Frisk?
No!
Stop the Nig
That's all that shit is.
Isn't it?

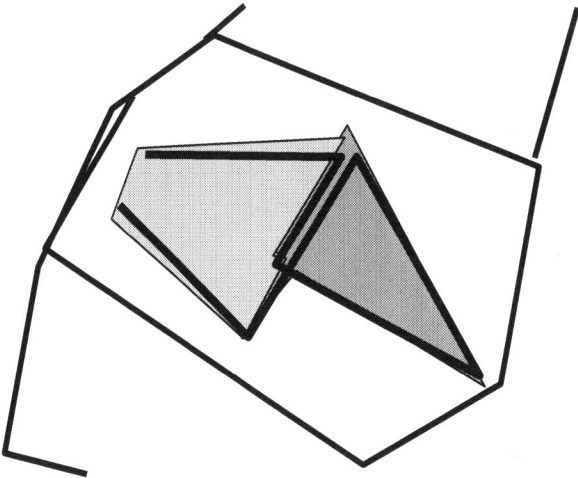

|D.A Huemæn|

<u>Name Change</u>
Human trafficking is another name for
trans-Atlantic slave trading.

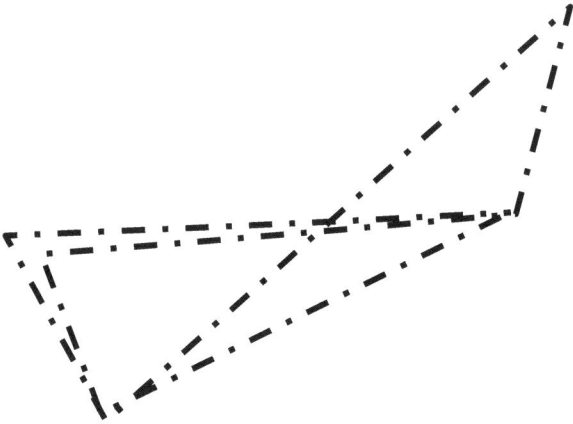

|D.A Huemæn|

I Feel
What is this I feel?
The heaviness in my heart
may be steel.
The loathsomeness of my thoughts
make me squeal
like a rat.
Like a rat on a trap
defenselessly watching the cat crawl closer
before it attacks.
What is this I feel?
Just a minute ago I was fine.
Yet a minute after
I am pulling my hair losing my mind.
What is this I feel?

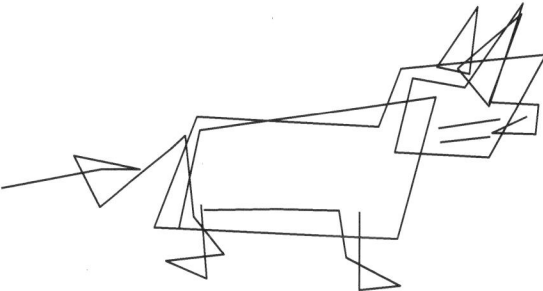

|D.A Huemæn|

<u>Synophobia</u>
Never would he join us.
Never would he call us.
Never would he write us.
His philosophy incorporated
none of these actions.
His philosophy says:
"Screw those Niggas.
You're not one of them.
You are your own entity,
like an island in the Atlantic sea
or like the *Parr*, *Diligent*, *Brookes*
You are yourself."
Does divide and conquer ring a bell?
He believes our struggles are not his own.
As if the oppressors would not
caste us on to the same boat.
They did it once for several hundred years.
Oddly enough many of us
Still don't get it.
If we fear togetherness,
We endanger our freedom.
Synophobia.

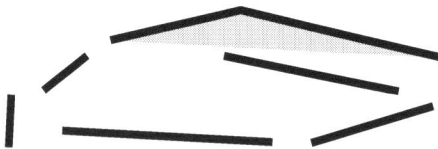

|D.A Huemæn|

Deep Deeper Deepest

I take a deep breath when I wake up.
I take a deeper breath before I sleep.
I take my deepest breath when
I'm about to close my eyes
I don't know
what the night has in store for me.
I take a deep breath when
I close my door.
I take a deeper breath
when I walk the streets.
I take my deepest breath
when I'm about to leave my house.
I don't know what my city has in store for me.
So it is deep, deeper, deepest,
just to maintain my sanity.

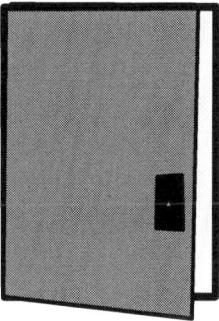

|D.A Huemæn|

Safeguard Your Heart
Don't play her at all.
What goes around
comes around.
It determines your cards.
Safeguard your heart.
Don't play her at all.
What goes around
comes around.

|D.A Huemæn|

<u>Don't Be Afraid</u>
Don't be afraid to be alone.
Misery loves company.
Stay at home.
Take a walk.
Stroll through your silence.
Don't be afraid to be alone.
Misery loves company.

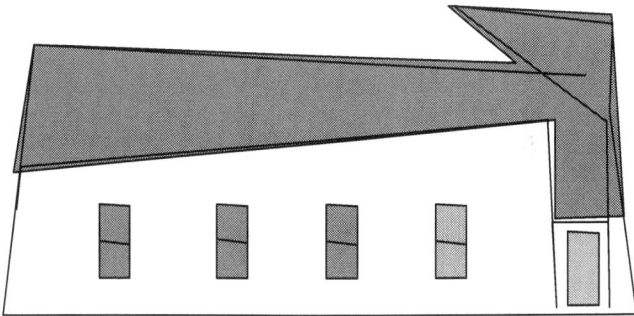

|D.A Huemæn|

Left Me to Die

They left me to die
I grew wings.
Now I fly.
Straight over their coffins.
Levelled up
Now my old death—
disturbs them at night.

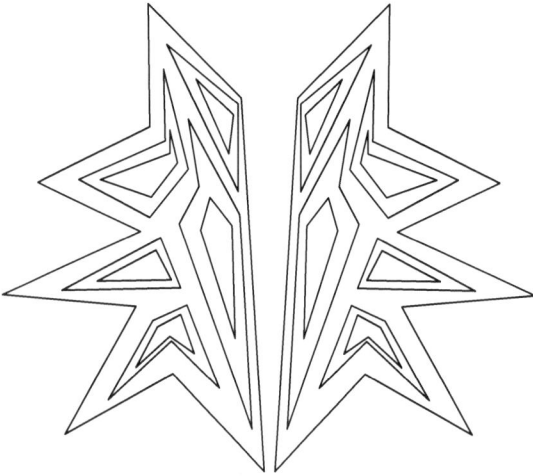

|D.A Huemæn|

<u>Thomian</u>
I want to see you
But you're never available.
You've loved me once.
Then consistently avoided the sequel.

|D.A Huemæn|

Chapter 5: Happiness

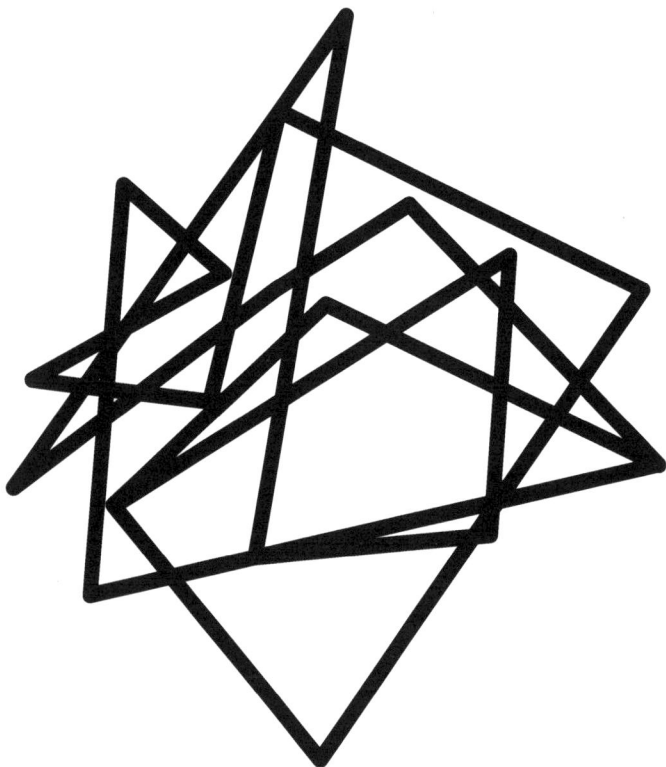

Cutie

You're a cutie patootie
With a big old African bootie.

|D.A Huemæn|

The Sun

The Sun went hiding
Behind a sea of shadowy clouds.
Then came out bright
And mightily proud.
Then calm—it shone...
Across all the Earth's rivers
Across all the Earth's trees
Across all the Earth's people
With the most ease.

|D.A Huemæn|

<u>The Earth Sings</u>
Have you ever woken up early
To hear the beautiful sounds
of the Earth at work?
During these hours
the clouds dance
to the rhythm
of the wind.
Birds perched on the branches of swaying trees
chirp to the beat of rustling leaves
as those leaves leave and fall to the green Earth.
Grieving men smile happily.
Solid waves crash against rocks
and restore mental clarity.
This is why I wake early.
The Earth sings and dances to its own melody.

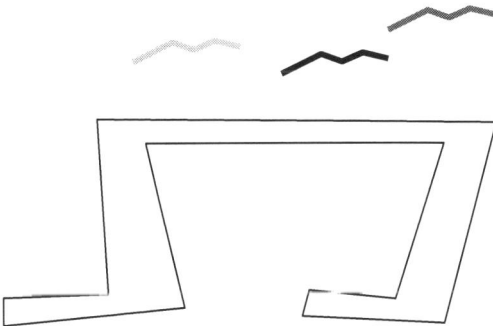

|D.A Huemæn|

<u>Worst</u>
break to take a breath.
Close your eyes to relieve the stress
Open your eyes and believe with your heart
In this world
You're not the worst
but the best
And yet you're not better
Than anyone else.

|D.A Huemæn|

<u>Blessing or Curse</u>

It is true everything happens for a reason.
Blessings and curses happen every season.
You see them but do you believe
Whether blessing or curse
is meant to be?

|D.A Huemæn|

My Journey

My journey to my goals
Don't end with this opportunity.
I see it not as backing down.
I see it as taking a different route.

|D.A Huemæn|

Scout from Bug

I'm that little scout from Bug.

That's probably why I am treated like a roach.

Scouted for a prison cell by the popo

"Po' people are worth less."

That's what they say.

Po' people go home

Into their cages.

Popo po' too

They po' in a different wayzes.

They don't understand

everything that exists today

tomorrow changes.

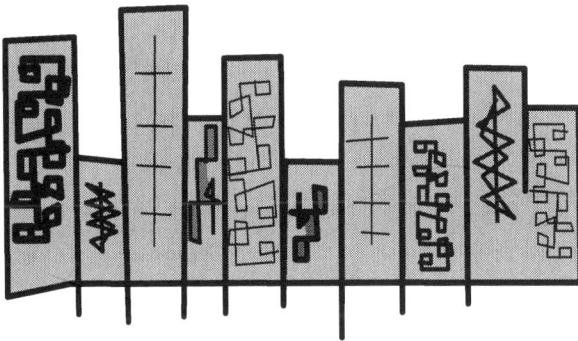

|D.A Huemæn|

I Wonder

I wonder if I wrote
Happy words
If I would be happier.
Or if I had happier friends
If I decided to close my eyes
And wished for a life
Of happiness
Would then it happen?
I'll just start here
With words on a page
And fears nowhere near.
Today I'll chose happiness.

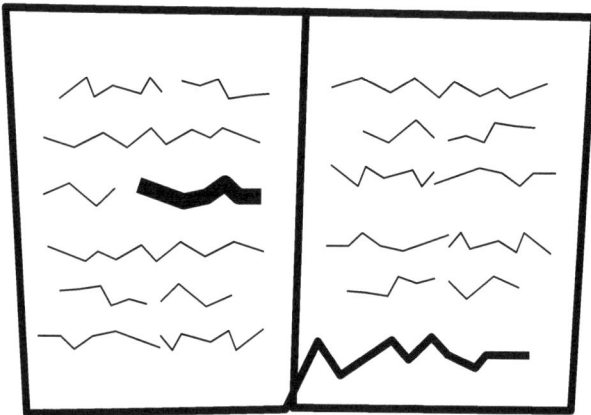

|D.A Huemæn|

Love is Free

When you love someone
You must allow them to leave.
Love is free.

|D.A Huemæn|

<u>3:30</u>

3 Hours and 30 minutes

Do you know what that is?

At my job it's about 140 cash

At my school it's approximately

1 ½ classes

At my home it is 3 ½ paintings.

|D.A Huemæn|

You Cried

Remember the nights you cried
Because you didn't want to be the person
You saw on the outside.
You committed to becoming great
And changed your fate.
Leaving few remnants
Of your lesser self.
Only pictures of you during a certain time
In a certain state
Hint at the conditions of your mental health.
Remember the nights you cried
Because you wanted to fly
Well my dear son,
Look what you've become.
You're the one.
And you're soaring high.

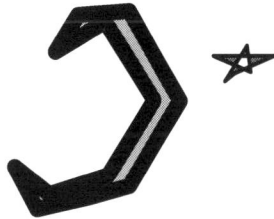

|D.A Huemæn|

<u>When I Dream</u>
I am untouchable when I dream.
That's why I dream.
I can fly when I dream.
In my dreams
not even the sky can limit me.

So I dream.
I dream until I'm eye to eye with the stars.
It feels great to dream.
So I dream about things
I want to come about.
Things I haven't seen
Though I know one day I will.
When I dream
I am untouchable when I dream.
Incredible, Invincible, Impeccable when I dream.
So I wake and believe
In my dreams.

When I Dream
I am untouchable when I dream.
That's why I dream.
Because I can fly when I dream.
In my dreams.
Not even the sky limits me.
So I dream.
I dream until I'm eye to eye with the stars.
It feels great to dream.
So I dream and believe.

ME
SKY

|D.A Huemæn|

<u>I Think</u>
I think I feel it.
I think I feel what so many wished they'd felt
but I'm not sure yet.
All I can say is that I think I feel it.
We've only been friends for a month and a half
but I think I feel it.
I hope what I think I'm feeling is true.
I think I feel it.
I hope you do too.

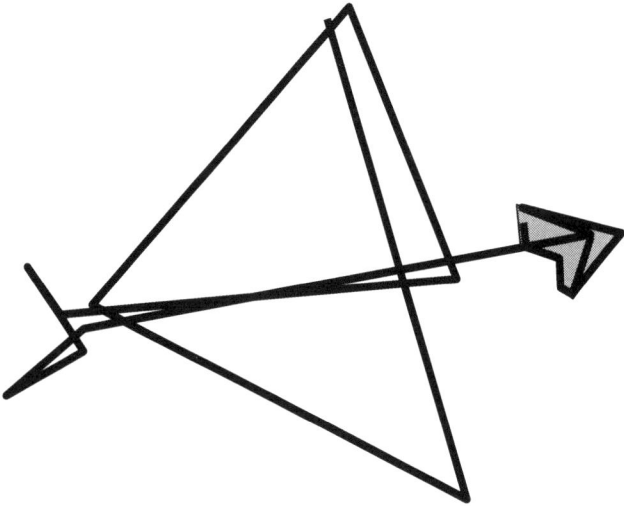

|D.A Huemæn|

I'm Blessed
I'm blessed and I'm cursed.
I am blessed to be Black.
But, sometimes my Blackness hurts me.
Only 14 years old
and already I've had 15 run-ins with the police.
Though, as sure as the racism hurts,
I'm more blessed than I'm cursed.

|D.A Huemæn|

Little Engine
The little engine that could.
Did.
Alhamdulillah

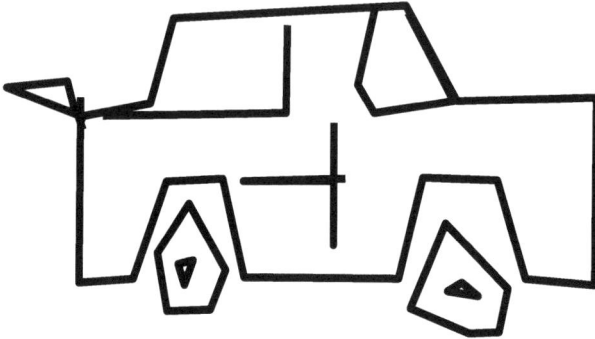

|D.A Huemæn|

You're There

I can tell you how much I love you.
I can show you how much I care.
I don't know how much I need you.
But whenever I do you're always there.

|D.A Huemæn|

Petals of the Sun

Petals of the sun
like splinters of hope
Bathe forever
In the minds of folks
Who wake up at 5
to smile and soak up the golden glow
from the sky that yokes our emotions with the tides
And the tides with the moon
And the moon with our food.
And soon you'll see
how it comes right back to you.
Petals of the sun
like splinters of hope
Show us everyday
how we are all looped together.
Just thought you should know.

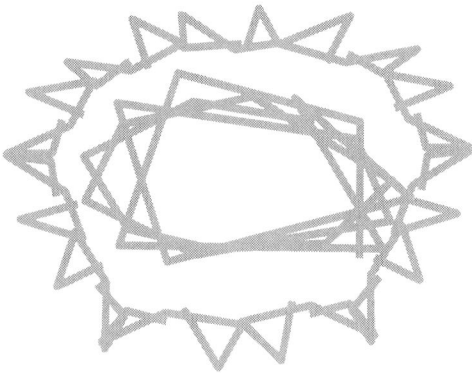

|D.A Huemæn|

<u>Challenge Accepted</u>
Self-defeating attitudes rejected
Teleprompt the technicals
To traverse this whole wide world
With full acceptance
That you are who you are
And that's how it'll be.

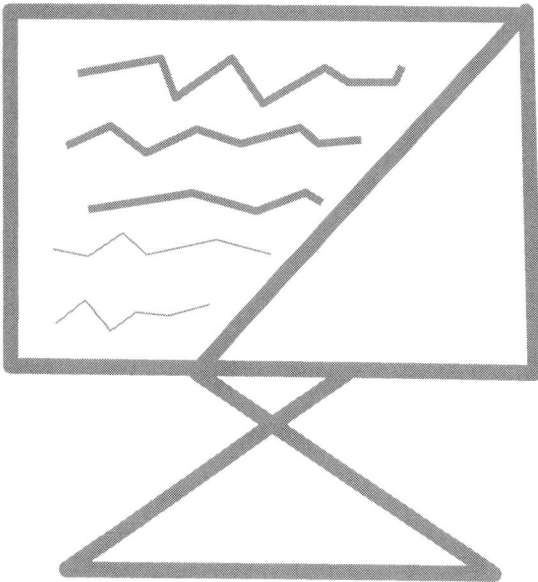

|D.A Huemæn|

I Rather

I rather live in the projects with my family.
Than sleep on a couch in midtown
I rather live in the projects with my family.
Than jet set around the world single.

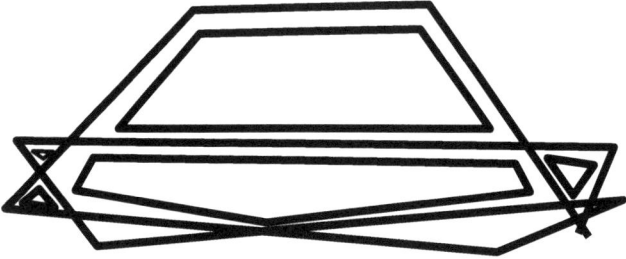

|D.A Huemæn|

Stone

I don't blame you.
You dodged a stone on a roll.

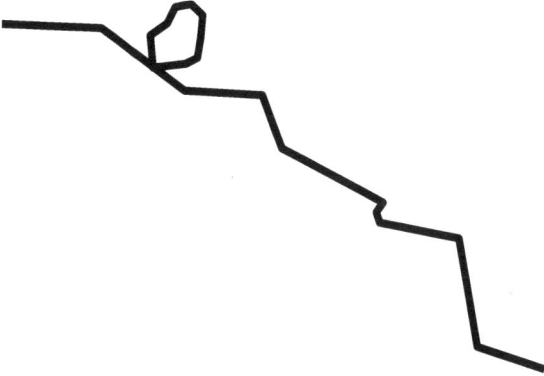

|D.A Huemæn|

Court the Queen
Court the Queen
The one who is "hard to get."
When you get her
Don't you forget
Your initial level of commitment.

If each day you match it.
You'll forever be winning.
Forfeit a life of smiling hearts
If you take her for granted.

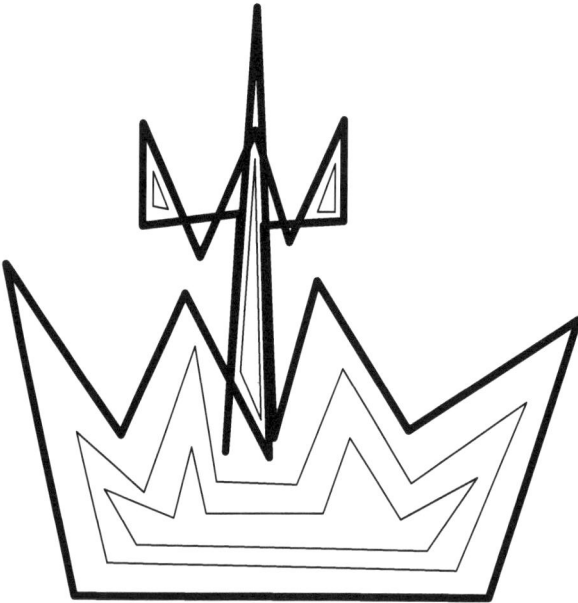

|D.A Huemæn|

Tonight

Tonight is a write night.
Tomorrow is a write day.
Tomorrow night…
You got it right
We're writing all week.

|D.A Huemæn|

Not There

I'm not there yet

But I'll be there soon.

If my words are hot air

Then my life is the balloon.

Defying gravity to take

A better look at

The different phases

Of the moon.

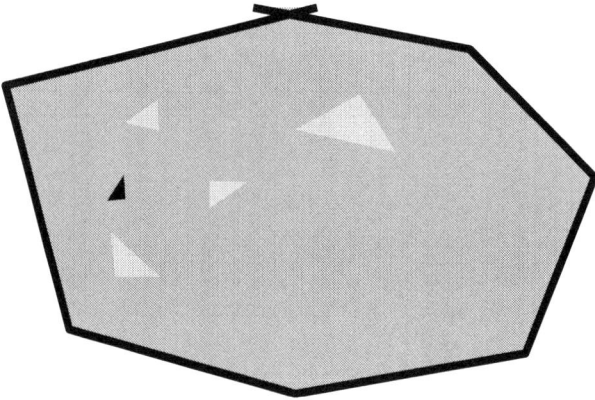

|D.A Huemæn|

Chapter 6: Sadness

Love?
What is love?
Is it something to say
Or do?
What is love?
Is it lie
Or truth?
What is love?
Is it in me
Or only you?

|D.A Huemæn|

<u>Uglier Child</u>
Yes, I am the uglier child.
The child that they do not love.
My dark skin shines bright
but they do not want me.
I am the uglier child.
But only in their eyes.

|D.A Huemæn|

I Can't Fight

I can't fight the feeling.
I don't know what to do.
I know I love you deeply.
I just think.
I can't be with you.

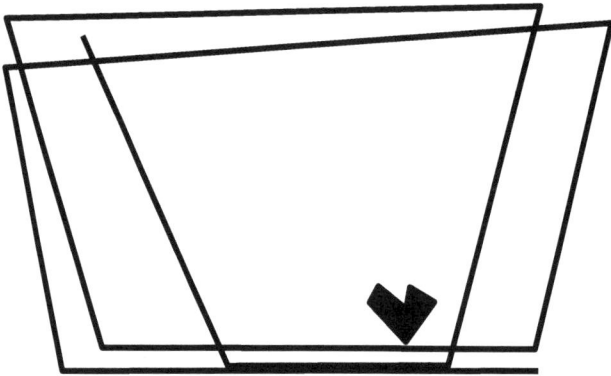

|D.A Huemæn|

Open Sea
I'm thinking of memories
of our late happiness
and youthful energies.
I'm thinking of what we used to be.
Times when I'd stare at you
You looking back at me.
Times when everyday was a new discovery
of all beautiful things in our open sea.
But we were blinded by our naivety.
Now all that's left is a shipwreck of memories.

|D.A Huemæn|

Want Happiness

I really do want happiness
but everything happening
makes me mad again.
Makes me wonder
What matters most
You and your problems
or me and mine?

|D.A Huemæn|

How Will I Succeed?
Stressed out from the mistrust that I've gained.
Blessed but all of my friends think I'm insane.
This shit is not a game.
My thoughts violently violate my brain.
In my dad's voice I hear:
"That's not gonna work.
Who cares?
I don't have time.
I can't make it there."
My mind replays
these words a million times
in my ears.
So I beg.
How will I succeed?

|D.A Huemæn|

<u>You Are Sad</u>

Woe is you who is glad only when others are sad.

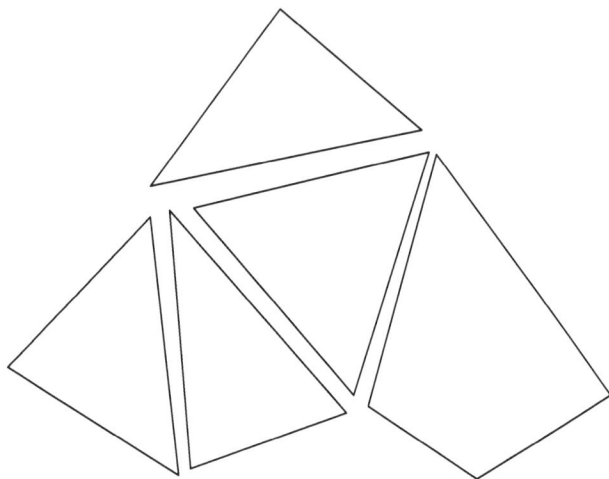

|D.A Huemæn|

<u>When I Die</u>
I am going to heaven.
That's a given.
I mean
It's the least I can get
For the hell
I've been imprisoned in.
I mean
At least I am well
With good health
And my dental is clean.
At least I can sleep.
Without creeps bothering me.
When I die
I am going to heaven.
 lest I survived
For a little bit.
I only hope
before I die
I would have made
A few people smile.

|D.A Huemæn|

Start Over

Sometimes,

I truly can't help but want to start over.

Redo a few moves

To remove the heaviness from my shoulders.

|D.A Huemæn|

I Love the Projects

I love the projects.
My pops can't get it.
He says only low-lives
drug dealers and convicts
Live there.
He's wrong.
My fears, cares, and dreams
Were born in the projects.
They still live here.

|D.A Huemæn|

She Said

She said she loves me.
I didn't know what to say.
The last woman I loved
took my heart and threw it away.
Now there's a hole
where I once felt things.
She told me she loves me.
I didn't know what to say.

|D.A Huemæn|

Homeless
Homeless by choice—kinda
I chose to move back to NYC
When I was 14.
I've been homeless ever since
while in this city.
I've lived on many couches
And behind a few.
But I've lived
And continue to.

|D.A Huemæn|

<u>Old Life</u>

I won't lie.

I miss my old life.

Why'd I leave that island?

I was wide-eyed green and wilding.

Trying to find my place in this new town.

On this financial capital

With no capital—

Just a pocket full of dreams I can't grab.

My hands filled with nightmares—

My friends' deaths.

I won't lie.

I miss my old life.

If I had a genie

I'd go back in no time.

I'd go back to

When Showtime was just a program on tv

And not 3 guys dancing on the 4 line.

I'd go back to

My feet bleeding on the street

Cause I didn't wear my flip flops.

I'd go back to

boys playing baseball

With tennis rackets.

(We ain't have it)

Girls playing hopscotch

Mongooses dashing.

Lizards are your ancestors

Returning to give their blessings.

The sea can be seen from every angle.

I miss my land.

The land of the free.

The place I'd looked to the ground

And see me.

Brown & green

The place I'd looked to the sky

 and see dreams.

That's word to everything.

The place I'd looked to the right

and see trees.

In all colorways

The place I'd looked to the left

 and see grandma's wealth—her health.

And love for all her kids.

I won't lie.

I miss my old life.

Why'd I leave that island?

|D.A Huemæn|

Missed Flight
I think about you each day.
Cutie you should've stayed.
It wasn't a direct flight
But I flew out the hood either way.

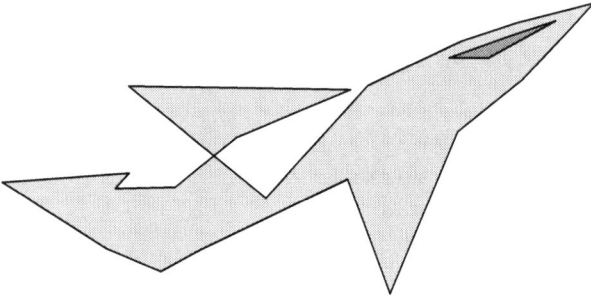

|D.A Huemæn|

Calloused Heart

You loathe me for getting whipped—and loving you.
Now I could get whipped and feel nothing.

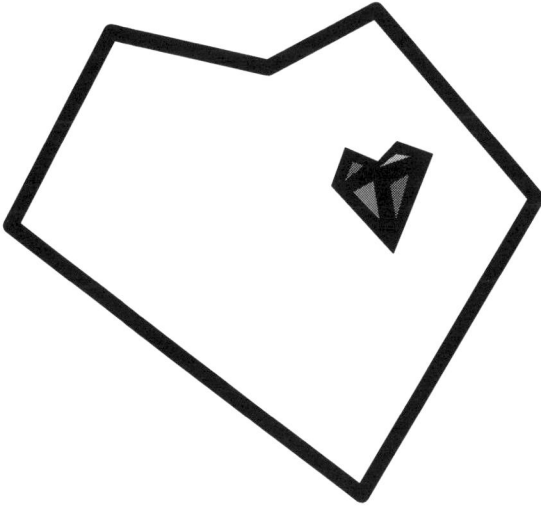

|D.A Huemæn|

<u>Blood Drips</u>
No love when you fight.
More blood when you love.

|D.A Huemæn|

Weird
Isn't it weird?
People's bodies are often available
but their presence isn't there.
It's better to do it alone.
Most people are too glued
To their phones.

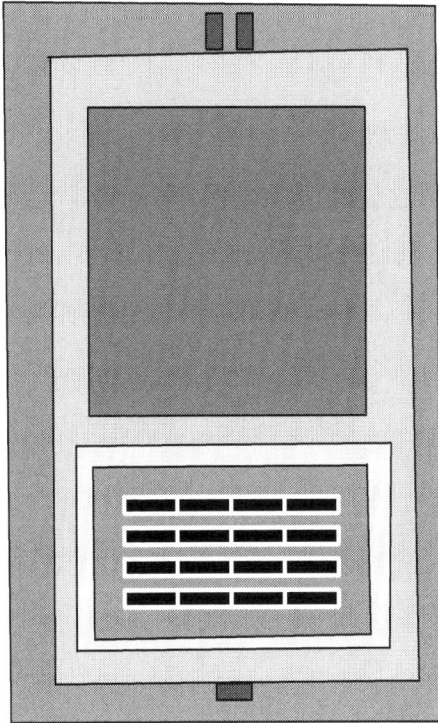

|D.A Huemæn|

<u>Listening</u>
I sat to eat
And got fed
With some truth—a sour truth.
Home boy was 18
Selling sour smoke.
I sat and chat for less
than a half hour
Listening to my Puerto Rican folk.
He spoke of the pain he felt and smelled on these shitty streets.
He said it was an acid shower.
He was flipping zapping power
And got booked.
Out now he is ends meeting as a cook.
Still smelling like shit though.
But no threats of getting cuffed...

|D.A Huemæn|

<u>Ms. Dee</u>
Fatima asked me
where is Ms. Dee
my answer chilled
like a cool breeze
over the Sand Sea
she was Kuwaiti
I am not.

|D.A Huemæn|

Heart of a Hoe
This heart can't be broken.
But it can be fixed.
A big bandage
is a Bad and Boujee Bittie.
Thick thighs
Thick titties
A bronze barbie
with a soft smile.

|D.A Huemæn|

<u>Pain I Feel</u>
This is the
I love you
You love me
But we can't be together
Pain I feel
This is the train
We derailed
The insanity kept still
The cold heat chills
Pain I feel.

|D.A Huemæn|

Chapter 7: Surprise

L Train

One woman's blessing
Is another's curse.
I sat on the L train
And saw exactly
This play out.
The conductor came on the intercom
And said this L train is
Skipping stops.
Next stop 105th
One woman exclaimed "Yes"
While the other became vex.

|D.A Huemæn|

<u>Think</u>
Do you ever think of how ~~big~~
Small you are?
Consider this then.
The Earth is the Milky Way
As a quarter dollar is to the United States.
Think about that for a second.
Now there are several neighboring galaxies
Comparable in size to our own.
Consider how small our Earth
Maybe among those collectively.
Now billions of people live on Earth
(which is like one quarter in the U.S)
How much smaller are ~~you~~ we?
And why are we so arrogant?

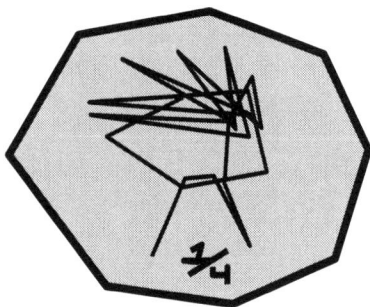

|D.A Huemæn|

Work

Hard work pays off
But can smart work pay better?
Some people work hard
And long
And others clever.
Some work all night
And never say never.
Some work by day
And avoid the weather
Others weather the weather
whether umbrella
Suede or leather.
Rain sleet snow
Hard workers are ready to go.

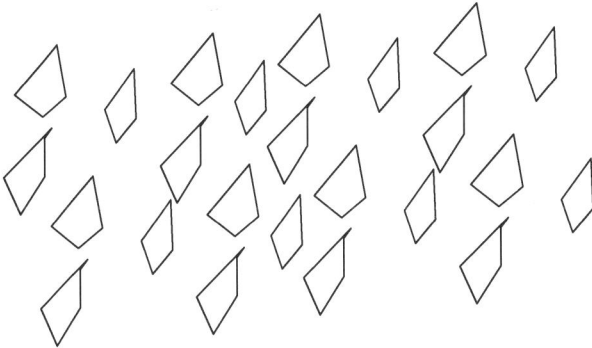

|D.A Huemæn|

The Old Woman

The Old Woman and the Corner
She was an old scruffy woman
who sat in her walker
She drank dark liquor
and smoked white killers alone on the corner.
But today, on 145th and Lenox Ave
for seven straight hours
a sip or a hit she did not have.
The first four hours a man of her tier sat and chatted.
Then at 3 o'clock a crowd formed around the addict.
The area outside the park
where the woman had sat down
had become an assembly of questioners
wanting to know what happened.

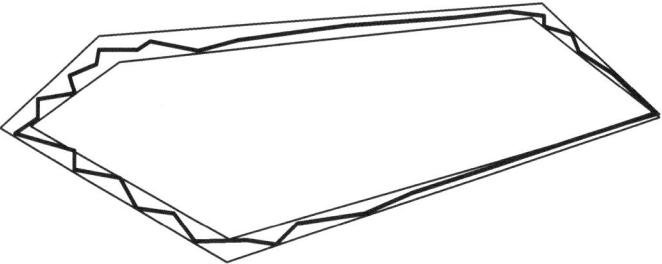

|D.A Huemæn|

Sex
Last night I had sex
In my grandmother's living room.
She didn't hear me.
Her only concern was
whether my cousin would follow in my shoes.

|D.A Huemæn|

Health

That $4 popcorn chicken box
Turns into a 40k medical bills.

|D.A Huemæn|

Test
6th grade?
Bro, you're a baby.
Don't test me
please don't test me.

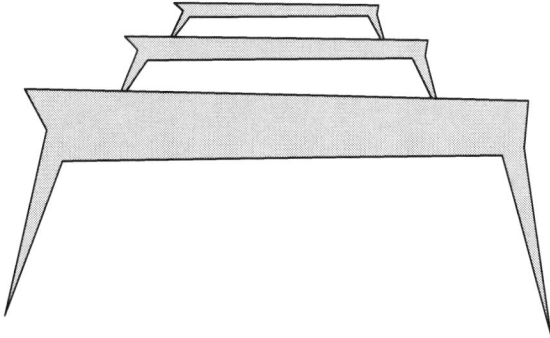

|D.A Huemæn|

Sweets

There's always sweets in life.
Life has plenty of candy.
But don't you eat too many
Unless you'd like cavities.

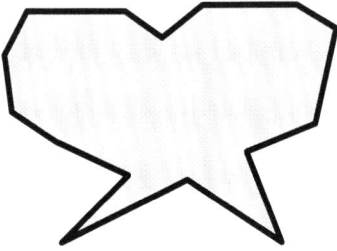

|D.A Huemæn|

Cards

The cards you get
aren't just the cards you get.
The cards you get
are also the cards you've dealt.

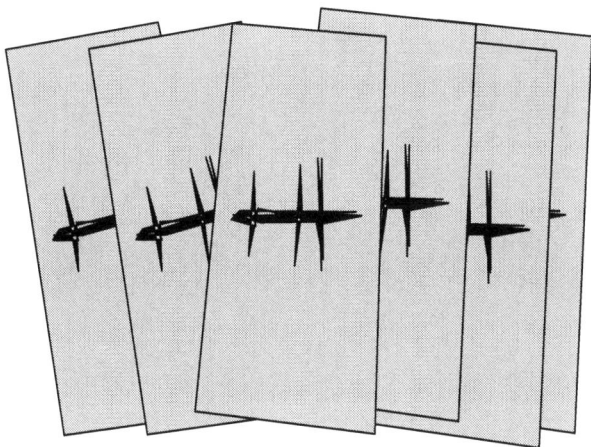

|D.A Huemæn|

<u>Produce</u>
Better a producer than a consumer.
Better a blooper than a non-shooter.

|D.A Huemæn|

We Lie
Men lie.
Women
Do the same thing.
The scale of truth
Moves
Always the right way.

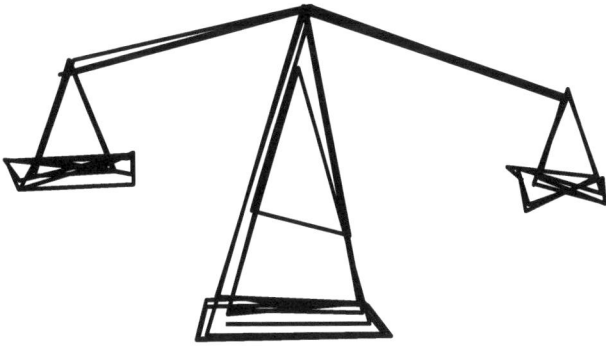

|D.A Huemæn|

My Hood

I'm building a spaceship to fly my hood out the hood.

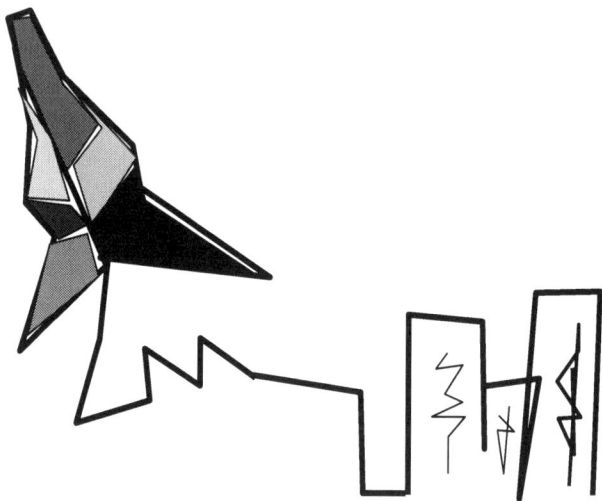

|D.A Huemæn|

Slow

I talk slow
I walk slow
I fuck slow.
I get money fast though.

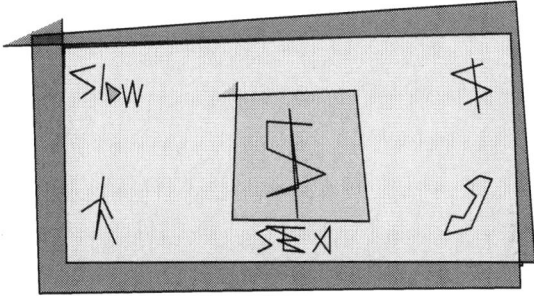

|D.A Huemæn|

Live
With something to live for
You don't die for nothing.
You don't die for anything
With something to live for.
You don't die for nothing
with something to live for.

|D.A Huemæn|

Worth

Your life is worth
Whatever you've lived for.

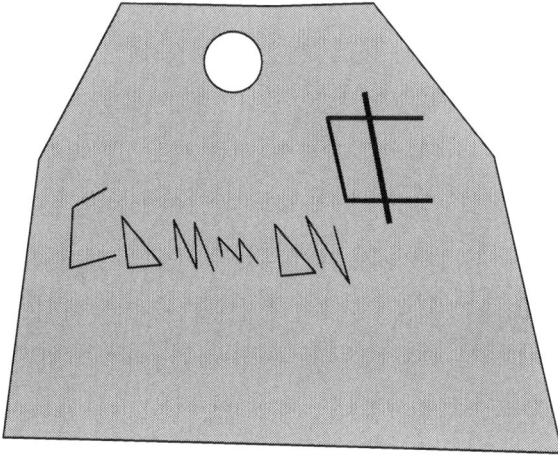

|D.A Huemæn|

Working

The only thing
Worth it is working.

|D.A Huemæn|

Chapter 8: Huemæn

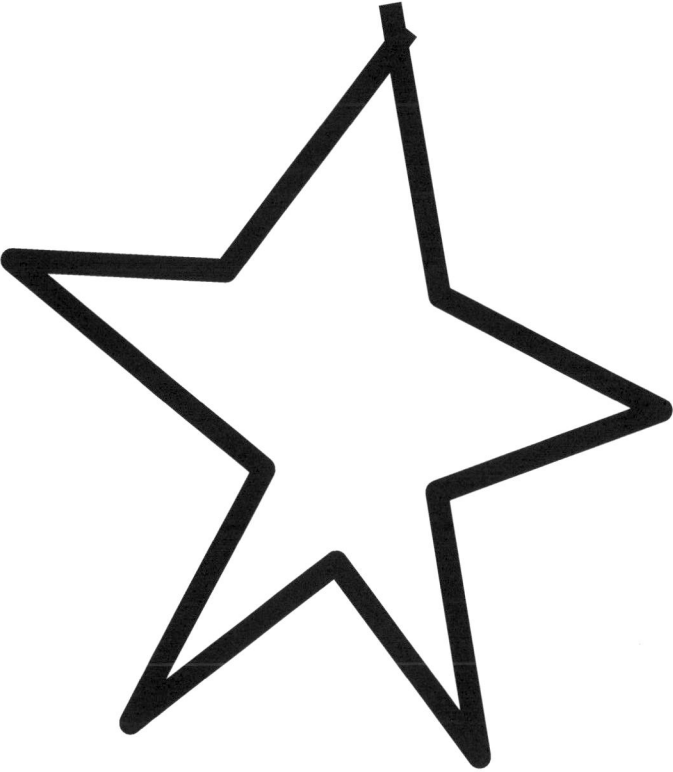

Sometimes

Sometimes I do
the wrong
Thing sometimes
I do nothing at all
Sometimes
I feel small
Sometimes
I feel tall
All and all
When I feel one way
10 minutes later
I feel another.

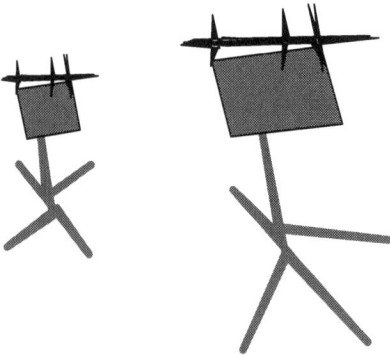

|D.A Huemæn|

<u>My Life</u>
My life is a poem
And a letter
Opened
To the whole world to see
Open to the whole world
And closed to me
My life everyone can read
Meanwhile I can't get a read
I need goals
About 3
Physical Emotional and Financial...

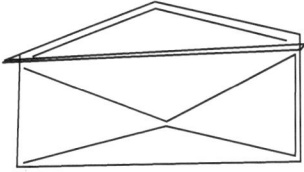

|D.A Huemæn|

No Pardons

I would say pardon my appearance
But I won't.
Just in case my students are home listening.
I don't need them to think
In order to get a ~~thought~~ point across
One must look a part.
One must fit the mold
Created and maintained by society's hold.
This only puts society in the driver's seat of the model U.
Our time on earth is our only luxury.
So waste it not on trying to be things you don't want to be.
Say what you want to say
Do what you need to do.
Love whom you want to love
Screw who you want to screw.
I would say pardon my appearance.
Or pardon this speech.
But I can't give two fucks.
You don't lie with me beneath my sheets.

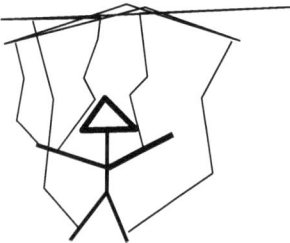

|D.A Huemæn|

Who Am I

I am a fallen soldier
making my way back to the top.
There are many in my neighborhood like me.
But many have been programmed to be trapped on the block.
If not trapped, like myself they've been profiled to be the target of cops.
If not profiled, they've been targeted to sell white rocks on the block.
Some have sold these white rocks to cops and found themselves trapped in a box.
Some have been shot and stabbed til their lifeless corpse lie in a box.
All just fallen soldiers predisposed to a lot.
Making our way back to the top.

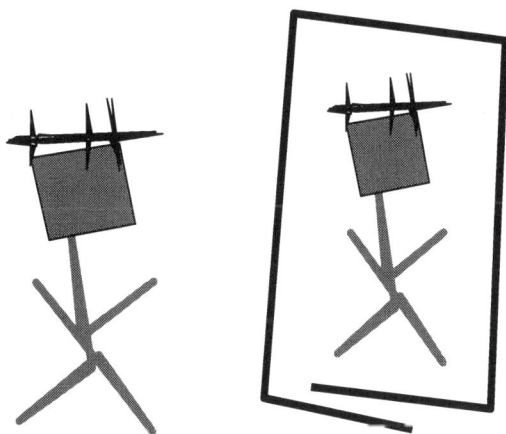

|D.A Huemæn|

<u>Sincerely Huemæn</u>
Dear Mr. Sam,
You may know me as "my nigga"
But my actual name is Huemæn.
I just wanted to say
You really got us good.
See, where I live
there are no neighbors.
The only thing I know is hood—
And a bunch of streets
Filled with loads of "my niggas"
Who all look like me.
You got us good Mr. Sam.
Sincerely, Huemæn

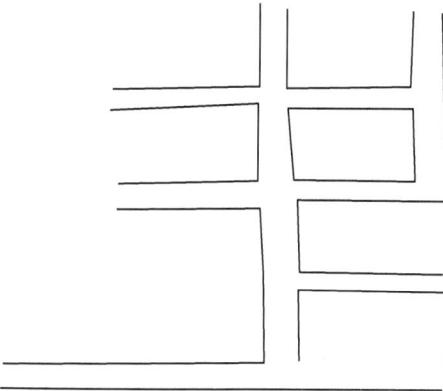

|D.A Huemæn|

Don't Say

Don't say stupid things to me
And think it's gonna fly.
I'm telling you right now
I'm not that kind of guy.
Sure my skin is chocolate.
And yes I made it through the trade.
But there is no way in hell
I'm gonna allow you to speak to me like a slave.
Speak to me like a king
And I'll speak to you quite the same.
Eye to Eye.
That's my mantra.
Otherwise don't say a thing.

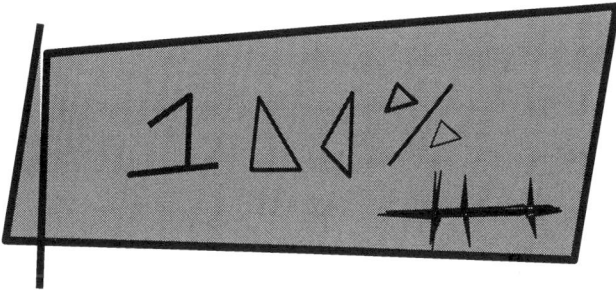

|D.A Huemæn|

Black Face
To you I'm just another black face
Up to no good.
I'm scheming to steal your purse
Because that's what we do in this hood.
I make you uncomfortable
Because you think I'm a convict.
But there is no racism involve
You think we're all criminals.

To you I'm just a black face
Up to no good.
But for my family
I'm the breaking of a 400 year curse.
Education is sacred.
Not only did I graduate
But I did it from this basement.

|D.A Huemæn|

On Becoming King

How are you little prince?
I heard that you would like to be king one day.
So, today your training begins.
It may sound cliché
but without a minute for play
let us start training with no delays.
Imagine your throne.
Imagine your sword.
Imagine your crown and your robe.
Impress these on your mind.
Recite "I am a king"
in the mornings, noons, and nights
and you will surely become a king
in all your glory and majestic might.

|D.A Huemæn|

Pray no Prey
Have you ever knelt to pray
That one day you'll be king?
That one day you'll get your crown
And no longer be prey in the U.S.A?

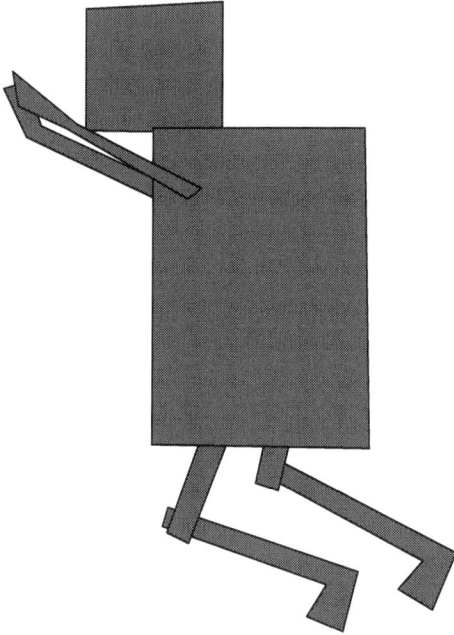

|D.A Huemæn|

<u>Write</u>
You don't have to like
what I write
I write for the fight
Not the likes.

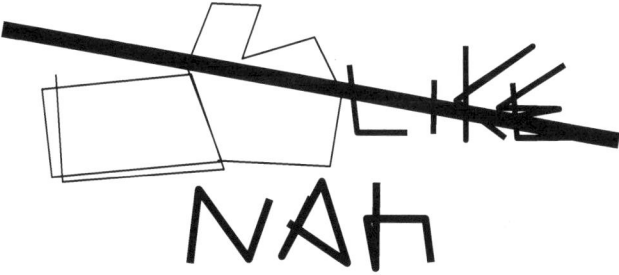

|D.A Huemæn|

Tied

A part of me wants to be tied to something.
Another doesn't.
My ancestral roots spent too long in bondage.
That Another
Is probably my great great great grand cousin grumbling.
"Cuzo if you get trapped
Imma beat your soul till it's black and blue…
You'll gain some sense and learn from your roots.
Family is the only thing you ought to be tied too."

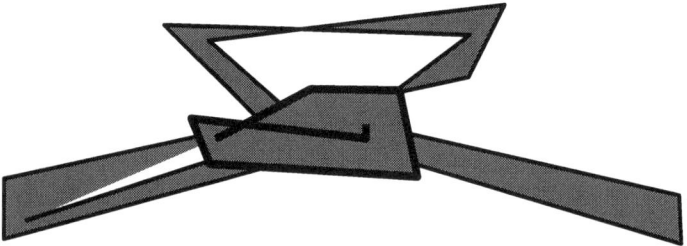

|D.A Huemæn|

Focal

Neither money nor sex is the focal point of my life.
However, each day I have this urge to fuck a dime.
Then I think damn.
I may as well use my mind and hands
For something more worthwhile.

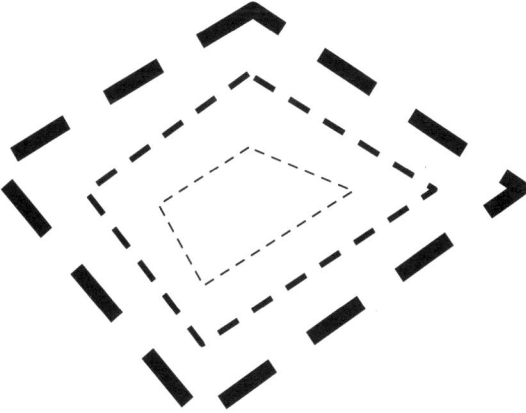

|D.A Huemæn|

Shapeshift

Teaching these kids
make me feel bipolar
times ten
viginti-polar –if that exists.
Principle Swift.
Look how many shapes I shift.

|D.A Huemæn|

I'm a Mæn

They call me a Dog.
I'm a Mæn.
They want me to sit
When I stand.
They want me to stand
When I kneel.
All these commands
Can't be real.

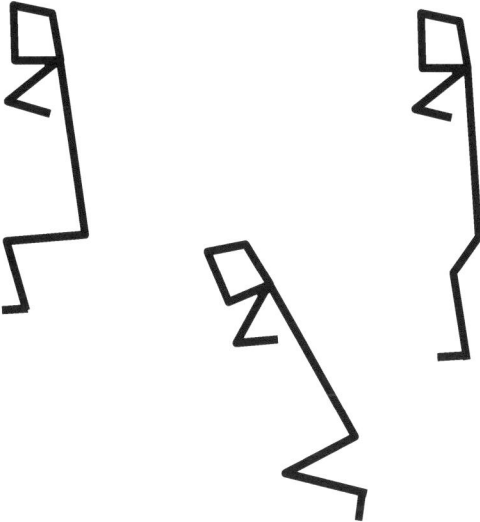

|D.A Huemæn|

I Soar
Sometimes I soar high
for a broader view.
Sometimes I fly low
To see the truer you.
I glide over riverbeds
For my reflection too.
Then vanish to the clouds
On the Wind's cue.

|D.A Huemæn|

<u>To God be the Glory</u>
I can't lie. I am blessed passed the sky.
Alhamdulillah

|D.A Huemæn|

Afterword

Thank you for reading this book. I truly hope you've found value in the poetry and prose I've shared with you.

If you have any questions, please feel free to reach out at **www.dahuemaen.com.**

Additionally, please take a moment to post a review online at www.Amazon.com, www.GoodReads.com, or wherever you managed to find this book.

Thank you for your time. I bid you a long life of good health and great happiness.

Sincerely,

86385258R00094

Made in the USA
Lexington, KY
11 April 2018